⸺THE BATTLE OF OUR GENERATION⸺

הרב אהרן פלדמן
RABBI AHARON FELDMAN
421 YESHIVA LANE, APT 3A, BALTIMORE, MD 21208
TEL.: 410-6539433 FAX: 410-6534694
STUDY: 410-4847200 EXT. 114
E-MAIL: RAF@NIRC.EDU

ROSH HAYESHIVA   ראש הישיבה
NER ISRAEL RABBINICAL COLLEGE   ישיבת נר ישראל

בס"ד

HASKAMA

One of the salient differences between the Jewish people and the cultures of other nations is that the goal of Jews is to control their passions and appetites while the goal of other nations is to fulfil them. Many Jews are not aware of this and therefore permit themselves to indulge in various activities which are forbidden according to the Torah. One of these is the wasting of seed.

For this reason ▓▓▓▓▓▓▓▓ has written a book for his fellow Jews showing that this act is forbidden according to the Torah and how refraining from it will add sanctity to a Jew's life. He also offers practical advice to those unfortunately caught up in this behavior which will help them control themselves.

I hope this book will have its intended effect and that will reduce the occurrence of this sin and will thereby cause sanctity to dwell amongst the Jewish people.

With blessings,

Aharon Feldman
Rabbi Aharon Feldman

─THE BATTLE OF OUR GENERATION─

בס"ד

Torat Hayim
1210 South La Cienega Blvd. Los Angeles, CA 90035 ☎310-652-2626 📠310-652-6979

א"ר יוחנן שלשה מכריז עליהם הק"בה בכל יום על רווק

הדר בכרך ואינו חוטא (פסחים קיג)

Maintaining the holiness and purity of the Neshamot of young people has always been a difficult task. In our generation it is an enormous challenge, but the rewards are monumental.

The Almighty Himself takes note of this!

It is a special pleasure for me to write these words to endorse this great work addressing this immense task, written by a young jewel in our community.

May this be a source of pride for the entire Los Angeles Jewish community.

Rabbi David Zargari

Rav of Kehilat Torat Hayim

----THE BATTLE OF OUR GENERATION----

Index

Preface..6

Why Fight?..8

Today's society is NOT normal!..............................11

Why is This the Most Difficult Test of Our Generation?.......13

How Does Pornography Destroy Families?....................14

A Different Form of Cheating....................................16

Finding the Perfect Soul Mate...................................17

The Selfishness of Masturbation................................17

9 Strategic Tips to Win This Battle.........................18-31

Inappropriate Dreams...31

How Pornography Damages Relationships..................33

One Can't Completely Hide From The Yetzer Hara........33

The Severity of Wasting Seed According to the Torah....34

Teshuva (Repentance)..35

Depression is Very Dangerous..................................37

Making it a Top Priority..37

How these Behaviors Lead to Addiction.....................39

How It Alters The Brain..40

Erectile Dysfunction..42

Japan Herbivores..44

Marriage is Not a Hospital......................................45

Power of 90..47

Think About it, Is It Worth It?.................................49

Conclusion...51

━━ THE BATTLE OF OUR GENERATION ━━

Congregation Aish Kodesh
of Woodmere
351 Midwood Road
Woodmere, N. Y. 11598
516 - 569-2660

RABBI MOSHE WEINBERGER

קהילת אש קודש דוודמיר

הרב משה וויינבערגער
מרא דאתרא

ב"ה

    Almost every day in my capacity as a community Rav as well as a Mashpia in Yeshiva, I deal with the tormented casualties of the battle of our generation. From bar mitzvah boys to men well on in their years, the unspoken affliction erodes the natural joy of life that should animate the existence of an observant Jew. The Yeshivas are filled with wonderful, sincere, and committed young men who are living lives of quiet desperation. Bochurim sit listlessly, feigning interest in a Tosafos or in davening, while their broken hearts have become incapable of absorbing the holy words. Sichos Mussar on the topic of spiritual growth cannot resonate with those who feel they are stuck in the mire of p'gam habris. Due to the shame and embarrassment associated with this matter, they rarely consult with an individual capable of guiding them in a wholesome, sensible, and halachik way. They remain oblivious to the wealth of advice found in authentic Torah sources, and have lost faith in their ability to control the most natural human desire. This state of silent despair often continues on in marriage, to the dismay of the young man who believed that marriage would cure him once and for all. Thus, the cycle of misery moves on with a bewildered wife destroyed as the unknowing and innocent victim of her husband's secret.

    I therefore see the publication of *The Battle of Our Generation* as a monumental breakthrough. A young ben Torah, making no scholarly pretenses, addresses the issue in a simple, honest, and direct way. Practical advice is offered from the sincere heart of a valiant warrior in this battle. I believe that fellow soldiers struggling in the trenches of our times will find renewed hope as they discover simple and effective weapons to be used in their efforts to find kedusha in their lives. I am so impressed with the undertaking of this remarkable young man who at his own expense has taken upon himself the responsibility to reach out to his peers with a simple resounding message; YOU CAN!

——THE BATTLE OF OUR GENERATION——

בס"ד

In *Kabbalah* every part of a person's body represents, and is deeply connected, to the spiritual world. When used in accordance with G-d's will those physical manifestations can have significant impact on the spiritual and physical well-being of both the individual and the world. If, G-d forbid, they are used negatively, then the opposite effect can also be true.

There is no more ostensive an illustration of this than the *Makom Habris* and the spiritual *Sefira* it corresponds to-- that of *'Yesod,'* meaning 'foundation' or 'essence.' This implies a direct correlation between the task of *Shmiras HaBris* and the quality of one's personal spiritual 'foundation'. If one is successful in its implementation, he will bring strength to his spiritual core. Failure will result in a foundation that is 'broken' or flawed, and then no matter how impressive the 'building' might be, it will eventually collapse. This is one of the reasons that the very first *Halachik* act in a Jewish male's life is that of *Brit Milah*. It defines at the outset man's essential task to strengthen himself spiritually by upholding the missive of *Shomer HaBris*. It is for this reason that the word *Tzaddik* is synonymous with S*hmiras HaBris* as well. In *Kabbalah*, Yosef is the Biblical character that represents the *Sefira* of *Yesod*. It is Yosef - *Shomer HaBris* in the incident of *'Eishes Potifar'* - that singularly ended up with the esteemed title of *'Yosef HaTzaddik.'*

In my work with young adults, I can attest that *Shmirat HaBris* is truly The Battle of our Generation. Time and again, I have seen that one entrenched in *pegam habris* finds it difficult, if not almost impossible, to properly connect to Hashem or feel true spirituality from his *Avodah*. As soon as one takes it upon themselves to work on this matter, they will find that the spiritual world opens up to them. Often they find that success in livelihood and relationships- especially marriage- generally follow. Given today's environment, many fear the task impossible. However, I have found that Hashem gives great assistance to those that call out to Him for help in this matter. You can, and will, prevail!

I can attest that the author is a true Oved Hashem who has already inspired many, and who will continue to do so through the outstanding efforts of this *sefer*.

With Great Admiration,

Rav Doniel Glanz
Mashgiach Ruchani
Yeshivat Shaarei Mevaseret Zion

----THE BATTLE OF OUR GENERATION----

PREFACE

Of all the battles we are forced to fight on a daily basis, which is the greatest battle? Which is the most important battle? Which battle is the most difficult? Which battle deserves most of our attention? Which battle is the battle of our generation? All of the great religious leaders today agree that the answer to all these questions is pornography and masturbation. That is the battle of our generation!

The reason that I have written this book is because I am aware of the fact that unfortunately the area of *Shmirat Habrit* (protecting oneself from wasting seed) has become the most difficult battle to fight in our generation. However, the saddest reality about this epidemic is that *Shmirat Habrit* remains unmentioned in both the secular and religious communities even though it is very prevalent. Organizations and Rabbis expound on many different topics and problems, yet one can go through his entire life never being educated about the dangers of masturbation. Most people are embarrassed to speak about pornography and masturbation, though ironically through education, one can find a cure to this epidemic. The purpose of this very book is to remove the taboo that surrounds this topic and to offer very practical advice to help one win the battle once and for all. This book is the product of several thousands of hours used to compile all the necessary materials to start a revolution. With God's help I hope that this will give people the necessary *Chizuk* and strategic tips to enable a person to not be a slave to his desires.

Chazal (our Sages of blessed memory) say the area of *Shmirat Habrit* is the "*Yesod*," (the foundation) of a Jew. The foundation of a building is underground remaining hidden and out of sight, yet, it holds up the entire building. If the foundation is weak then the building can collapse at any point. Similarly, *Shmirat Habrit* is also hidden from all others, aside from you and Hashem, yet it is our foundation.

----THE BATTLE OF OUR GENERATION----

If you are not *Shomer Habrit* then your foundation is weak causing your whole spiritual structure to be fragile.

This book is relatively short; yet, one cannot just read it as one would read a storybook. One who reads this proactively and constantly tries to implement the different tips and strategies can be assured that having picked up this book was one of his best life investments. All the material presented here is from various sources, ranging from our holy Sages to the leading modern day psychologists around the globe.

----THE BATTLE OF OUR GENERATION----

Why Fight?

Imagine you go with a friend to an ice cream store. You order cookies and cream with mint chocolate chip ice cream while your friend chooses vanilla. "Why vanilla?" you ask innocently. Your friend explains that while he has never tasted any other flavors he knows with absolute certainty that vanilla is the best tasting flavor. The truth is that if your friend had tasted other flavors he would have realized that there is much he is missing out on. A whole array of flavors are laid out before him, but he stubbornly refuses. Your friend is very much missing out!

This same concept applies to life itself. There are those that say "I am happy with where I am. I'm not interested in changing." Perhaps they are content. But are they missing out? They will never know because they stubbornly refuse to explore other options. In truth, a person of dignity will always be eager to learn new things as he is constantly seeking to improve his life and the world around him.

When we speak about sexuality most people have not simply considered what is truly possible. People give in to their sexual temptations and desires on a daily basis because they feel that the short-term physical pleasure they receive is the greatest pleasure possible. On the contrary, there is no better feeling than freeing oneself from being a slave to his desires. Only those who have achieved the strength to abstain from masturbation and watching pornography can attest to how much more fulfilling and meaningful life can be.

Shmirat Habrit has become, by far, one of the most difficult tests for our generation. The *Gedolim* (great Rabbinic leaders) of our generation have instructed that every male must prioritize working on *Shmirat Habrit*.

----THE BATTLE OF OUR GENERATION----

The results of this tragic epidemic lay clearly before us. The divorce rate in some cities in America has skyrocketed to an obscene **75%!!!** (California Court Statistics Reports) **That means 3 out of every 4 marriages are ending in court!**

A non-Jewish website designed to combat pornography and masturbation (fightthenewdrug.org) makes a shocking claim that 57% of divorces have to do with the husband's deep desire for pornography and masturbation during his marriage.

Shmirat Habrit has been a taboo topic in our religious communities for far too long. The very fabric of our society is at stake. Families are literally being destroyed. Rabbis and marriage counselors who are frequently involved in the marital issues of their communities can all attest to the fact that husbands, wives, and even children are being significantly impacted. The instant pornographic availability that the Internet provides has made our *Nisayon* (test) that much more challenging.

As Rabbi Yosef Viener from *Agudas Yisrael* Monsey said in a recent talk on family security: *"Not a week goes by that I don't have to deal with a Shalom Bayit problem (marital issues) or a problem in Chinuch Habanim, or a very fine Bochur who will call me up – or at least what is left of a very fine Bochur – calls me up crying, begging for help. There is nobody that can claim that either they're not affected, or a family member, or a neighbor, or the chaver sitting next to them in shul, or the chavrutsah sitting across from them in yeshiva. If you discounted it until now, you're going to have to take my word for it when I say that there is no bigger problem facing the yechidim in Klal Yisrael and communities at large than this. Nothing even comes close. There's an obligation to do something now before there's no semblance of Kedusha (holiness) left in Klal Yisrael and I don't say that lightly. Keep in mind, the people who come to me are so frum (religious) and so upset about what's going on, that they're willing to talk to their Rav. That means that there are thousands of people who would never even speak to their Rav."*

——THE BATTLE OF OUR GENERATION——

A common misconception among unmarried young men is that marriage will solve this problem. Rabbi Twerski (a world renowned Rabbi and Psychiatrist) has repeatedly taught that, **"Marriage does not solve the problem of addiction to lust; if anything it makes it even worse."** In fact, if one gets married without having already fixed this issue, it can ultimately destroy the lives of many people, instead of just one. For addicts who have learned to use lust to fill a deep inner void and as a solution to all of life's difficulties, their wives and children will never be enough for them.

Many marriage counselors say that this addiction is the main cause of *shalom bayit* issues (marital problems) and divorces amongst young couples today.

The first key to winning this battle is "acceptance." We need to accept that we have a problem and that **we need help.** Otherwise, as one reads through all of this he can constantly fool himself by saying, *"Maybe this is relevant to other people, but surely this does not apply to me!"*

People often like to think that they will live happily ever after and that their pornography and masturbation problem will in no way ruin their marriage. However, we must ask ourselves, "Did those who eventually got divorced ever think on their wedding night that they would one day get divorced?" Obviously Not! The point is that although everyone likes to think that their marriage will work out perfectly well, the statistics have shown us that a majority of marriages actually end in divorce. Unless we put in sufficient effort to eradicate the problem of masturbation, then we are no different than the average male who is at a very high risk of having marital issues and divorce.

In this modern day and age, we must all set the proper boundaries to totally eliminate this issue. This is one of the most effective ways to set ourselves up for a more successful marriage and life. Education and abstinence are critical for solving this challenge.

----THE BATTLE OF OUR GENERATION----

It is written in the holy Zohar, "No person should feel depressed, even should he be engaged all his days in this conflict (of *Shmirat Habrit*), for perhaps because of this was he created. This is his service – to constantly subjugate his *Yetzer Hara* (evil inclination)."

Today's Society Can No Longer Be Classified as Normal!

In modern times, it is very easy to be fooled by the belief that the world always looked the same in regard to society's moral compass. We often justify to ourselves that there is nothing wrong with today's society. However, nothing could be further from the truth. Our generation is immensely different than any other generation that preceded it in terms of morality.

Here are some examples to illustrate this point:

In the 1920's, it was very rare for a woman to reveal her ankles in American society. In fact, to many people, the very act of dressing immodestly was considered rude and unmannerly. Photographs from that period of time, of Jews and **even non-Jews**, support the fact that all women wore very modest clothing, as their skirts almost reached their ankles and their sleeves covered most of their hands. Today, society will look at any person dressed in such a fashion as 'weird' and in a negative way. Unfortunately, in today's society, a woman is perceived to be attractive when she dresses immodestly. Relative to the high standards of society for the past thousands of years, the last several decades has changed immensely.

In the middle of the 20th century, Lane Bryant was a woman who created a woman's clothing company. Later on, Lane wanted to put out an advertisement to attract expecting mothers to her clothing line. However, when she approached numerous magazines, not even one magazine was willing to place such an advertisement.

----THE BATTLE OF OUR GENERATION----

The New York Times felt that it was immodest to place an advertisement featuring a pregnant woman. To clarify, we are not talking about pornography here or even a scantily dressed woman; we are merely speaking about a photograph of an expecting mother. Yet, society had very high standards.

Now, imagine taking any of the 'normal' magazines that we have today, filled with all the types of photographs of scantily dressed women, and showing it to people in the mid 1900's. The people would boycott the magazine and protest against it aggressively. However, in our generation, these photographs are considered to be the norm and are accepted by the mass public.

Moreover, former American President, Herbert Hoover, made a public announcement in the 1930's saying, "It is the duty of our government to safeguard our children." Why did he make this announcement? The reason was that there was a new technology called the radio and since it would be broadcasted in people's homes, it was considered a huge danger that required monitoring.

Furthermore, when the initial Hollywood movies were created, the standards of ratings were extremely strict. Until 1967, there wasn't even a single publicly displayed movie that was rated "R". Suddenly, in 2001, 63% of all regular movies were rated "R". However, they were rated "R" for content that in the past, such as in the 1920's, would be considered X-rated and perverse. Additionally, in today's movies, only 1 out 7 sexual scenes is actually between a husband and wife — just imagine the messages that are subconsciously being conveyed into the minds of society.

In the 1960's, the Beatles' came out with a song in the Midwest that caused much uproar. There were large gatherings with huge crowds burning Beatle's records. But Why? What did they say or do to deserve this reaction from their fans? The reason was that they used lyrics that said, "I want to hold your hand!" America demonstrated as if its innocence was being corrupted. One of the band members, John Lennon, said in an interview, "One night on a show in the South somewhere somebody let off a firecracker while we were on stage. There had been threats to shoot us, the Klan were burning Beatle records outside and a lot of the crew-cut kids were joining in with them. It was that bad." (The New York Review)

In a very short span of time, America has gone from a normal, respectable nation to a very disturbed and lowly nation. As Jews, we have to understand that although morality for the gentiles might change from generation to generation, our eternal Torah which teaches us the truth, does not and will not ever change. The problem is that we live amongst such filth that it often affects us in thinking that everything is actually normal and justified. However, it is vital that we compare the modern world with the way society acted for thousands of years up until the recent generations. By making this comparison, it would become clear to us that our current generation is in fact disturbed and perverted. This comparison will allow us to understand the distinctions and fences we must make for ourselves. This will help us separate from the filth and remind us to not accept what society tries to coerce us to do.

In the early 1900's, the 6% divorce rate was considered to be a huge issue. Today, the divorce rate is at 60%, and in some places, it has even hit 75%. Affairs are as common as the common cold and we wonder why?

Why is this the Most Difficult Test of Our Generation?

Before the Internet took over the pornographic industry, one could only gain access to pornography by purchasing it in a store. This acted as a deterrent since one had to engage in an awkward face-to-face interaction with the seller. Additionally, the risk of being seen by others and ruining one's reputation served as another preventive barrier. These factors, coupled with the expense of pornography, created a culture where pornography was simply not so prevalent.

----THE BATTLE OF OUR GENERATION----

In the 1990's with the invention of the Internet, everyone began to have unlimited free access to pornography. Today, almost everyone has a smartphone that provides instant access to pornography whenever and wherever they find themselves. We have seen the pornographic industry grow from a multi-million dollar industry to a multi-billion dollar industry. Inflation aside, this is an unprecedented growth (New York Times Magazine).

How Does Pornography Destroy Families?

Pornography is harmful for many reasons. For now we will focus on only two critical elements:

Tolerance

1) A person who has never previously drunk alcohol will quickly become intoxicated by even a little amount of alcohol. Over time, as this person continues to drink he will build a tolerance for alcohol and need greater and greater amounts of alcohol to achieve the same level of intoxication that he initially felt with just a small amount of alcohol. Similarly, for someone who has not been exposed to a women's body, even seeing a scantily dressed woman may arouse him. However, if that same person begins to watch pornography, then overtime that scantily dressed woman will not be as arousing to him anymore. As one builds tolerance, he will begin to need more "intense" or "hardcore" material to achieve arousal. Similar to the alcoholic, this person has built a tolerance to pornography.

During marriage, no matter how attractive or alluring the wife is, the "tolerance" is already in place. Real life can never compare to the pornographic inspired fantasy he has built in his mind. His wife will never be able to compete with the fake Photoshopped film actresses and he will not be satisfied with what she offers. Pornography thus leads to a cheapening of the sexual gratification of marriage. Sadly, we live in a time where this often leads to marital disharmony and divorce.

––THE BATTLE OF OUR GENERATION––

Unrealistic Expectations

2) As previously mentioned, pornography is a multi-billion dollar industry and it has unfortunately become sexuality for the digital generation. Producers of pornography regularly use Photoshop so the women seem more attractive than they actually are. Adult film actors and actresses are paid to exaggerate the pleasure of sexuality in order to provide a more enticing product for their audience. The audience may enjoy the film but what they are left with is an unrealistic expectation of intimacy. The reality of sexual intimacy is that it's a beautiful part of marriage but it is far from the picture that is painted by pornography. Consider the impact it will have on one's marriage when on his wedding night he finds himself disappointed by all the "blemishes" of his spouse.

Was the momentary pleasure of pornography worth it? After all, no sexual experience could possibly live up to the hype they have portrayed on screen. Please don't misunderstand. A marriage built on shared values; a marriage built with true love, compassion, dignity etc…will have a much more dynamic and profound intimacy than anything the pornographic industry could possibly portray. However, it will be one based on connection not fiction. How devastating is it that a husband may even momentarily think, "Perhaps my wife isn't what I hoped for." What a tragic impact this may have on the marriage.

Consider this from the women's perspective; she has done nothing wrong. She may be a devoted wife and a loving mother, but she cannot live up to the unrealistic expectations of her husband's pornographic imagination.

How many wives feel inadequate in the bedroom because their husbands are somehow never satisfied? The unsatisfied husband may even (God-forbid) leave his wife but the pornography problem lies within and therefore will follow him from marriage to marriage.

----THE BATTLE OF OUR GENERATION----

Marriage is one of the most important relationships in one's life. The question is: do you want to sacrifice the potential pleasure of a truly happy and intimate relationship for the temporary pleasure of pornography and masturbation? Why would you put that happiness in jeopardy for a mere moment of satisfaction?

A Different Form of Cheating

Cheating in marriage has been taught to us in the wrong way. Cheating does not only constitute of one who physically engages in intercourse with a women other than his wife. In fact, the reality is that if one imagines another woman while he is engaged in intercourse with his own wife, then he too is to some degree cheating. How would you feel if your wife was imagining other men while married to you? If one is filling up his brain with these images and videos, then he should be certain that they will be so deeply ingrained in his mind that they may resurface during the action of intercourse. Therefore, one must cleanse his mind of these images completely to avoid this problem.

A part time marriage counselor and professor of psychology at UCLA quoted one of her patients saying, *"A wife finding her husband with another women is easier to accept, after all the other women may be younger or prettier. But for a man to prefer masturbation than sexual intimacy with his wife really twists the knife of rejection on her back, and the memory decades later is still etched into her mind and it breaks her self esteem."*

Even if you consider yourself a virgin when you get married, the fact remains that if you have masturbated a lot, your wife will not be the only person whom you have experienced sexual pleasure with. The most you could do is to put in real effort to never do it again. That way the memory of the times you did this will not be so fresh in your mind and the temptation will fade eventually. The less you have masturbated and the longer ago it was, the less of a threat it will be to your sexual exclusivity in marriage.

––THE BATTLE OF OUR GENERATION––

Finding the Perfect Soul-Mate

How does Hashem coordinate which two people will get married together? The Torah teaches, "אין מזווגין לו לאדם אשה אלא לפי מעשיו" (Sota 2a). This means that a person is only set up with a woman based off of his actions. Rashi comments "Prootzah Lerahsha" meaning a wicked man will get an immodest woman "Vetzenooah Letzadik" and a righteous man will be matched up with a modest woman. In other words, you get what you earn!

There are those who think that their immodesty is perhaps a problem of the moment but it will in no way affect their future. *Chazal* teach us that this is simply not true. Hashem judges our behavior in determining who is an appropriate match for us in marriage. Hashem takes note of a person who constantly puts in the effort to stop watching pornography and wasting seed and such a person is guaranteed to merit a better wife. As marriage is one of the most central relationships of a person's life, it would be foolish to behave in a manner that will leave one with an immodest wife.

The Selfishness of Masturbation

Marriage is all about giving. In fact, the Hebrew word for love, אהבה, comes from the Hebrew word הב which means to 'give'. The main way to love another is by giving to them. In every Jewish book about marriage, the word that will constantly repeat itself is "give." As long as both the husband and wife are focused on giving to the other partner in the marriage, then in reality, both end up receiving. However, if each partner begins to focus on his or her own needs, then it becomes like a game of tug of war and neither partner truly gains in the marriage.

Masturbation is exactly the opposite of giving. In fact, masturbation is an extremely selfish act. A person who masturbates constantly trains himself to feed his own sexual desires as soon as they come by, reinforcing this self-centered way of thinking. When that same person gets married, it may be very difficult for him to play the most important role in a marriage, which is to be a giver. Masturbation gratifies only one's own sexual desires, a characteristic which can surely carry over into the marriage and result in unhealthy intimacy.

9 Strategic Tips to Win This Battle:

When confronted with war, both sides must make sure to use the most sophisticated weaponry and tactics to defeat the enemy. Our *Yetzer Hara* comes fully equipped to the battle with the most modern technology available. However, the problem is that many times we enter the battle unarmed and set ourselves up for failure. To win this battle we too must enhance our arsenal and review our tactics in order to maximize the possibility of success.

Tip #1 –Shmirat Einayim

Perhaps the most important tip in conquering our lust and becoming a person that is *Shomer Habrit,* is that we must monitor what we look at. There is a famous quote that teaches, "You can't lust for that which you don't see." Yes, this tip may seem very obvious; but most people are not careful enough. Someone who is eager to lose weight would be greatly challenged if he works at a fast food restaurant. A recovering alcoholic would be foolish to work at a bar. We too cannot expect to win this battle if we are constantly being confronted with inappropriate images.

Instead, one has to be proactive and make sure that he is not at risk of falling. The best way of doing this is by setting up fences for oneself. For example, if one thinks that certain friends on their Facebook tend to post pictures that aren't the most appropriate, then he should be proactive and hide posts from that friend. If one tends to browse websites that are not good for him, then he should understand that he requires Internet filters to prevent him from seeing things that will cause him to slip up.

----THE BATTLE OF OUR GENERATION----

The Mishna in *Pirkei Avot* (Ethics of our Fathers) teaches, "Who is the strong one? The one who conquers his temptations." (4:1) Many times people think that it is below them or close-minded to close their eyes when they see something inappropriate either in the streets, on the computer, or in a movie. However, those who are not willing to change the channel for two minutes until the inappropriate scene goes away or the one who sees an inappropriate billboard but does not look away is really the one that is 'close-minded', as he is setting himself up for failure. That person tells himself, "its not going to do anything to me." Even if that person does not end up wasting his seed right then, the next time when he's home alone, that image that was etched in his mind will resurface and can cause him to transgress.

People dedicate so much of their time physically working out in order to look strong and fit in the eyes of others. Some people put on a show to find favor in the eyes of others by acting brave and strong. The truth is that making God impressed with us is tremendously more important and significant than impressing humans that are mere flesh and blood. According to our Torah, real strength in the eyes of God is when one conquers his temptations or when one at least puts the time and effort into fighting this battle of our generation.

Even though setting up fences helps tremendously and is definitely a requirement to conquer the battle of *Shmirat Habrit*, every person will often bump into something inappropriate, as one cannot live in a box. For instance, one could be waiting by a traffic light and a scantily dressed woman can walk right in front of his car. However, it is completely up to him to decide whether he wants to continue to look at that woman or rather to look away. If he decides to look away, not only is he rewarded spiritually but he also makes it significantly easier to ultimately conquer his temptations. The first look sometimes isn't up to us, but after that, we have the full capability to not look further.

——THE BATTLE OF OUR GENERATION——

It is also forbidden from the Torah for a man to stare at a woman as we repeat 3 times daily in the Shema, "You shall not stray after your heart and after your eyes." (Bamidbar 15:39) The heart and eyes are two agents of sin, since the eyes see, the heart desires, and the body commits the sin.

The Gemara (Yoma 74b) says that the *Yetzer Hara* prefers to make one sin through sight rather than through physical sin. The reason for this is that the *Yetzer Hara* fears that by physical sins one will feel remorse and do *Teshuva* (repentance) but for sins of sight one tends to not do *Teshuva* nor regret his actions.

There is also a fundamental difference between seeing something vs. focusing on it. When we drive on the freeway, we see many different light poles but we don't focus on them and thus, soon after, we aren't thinking about them anymore. The same is true with regards to accidentally seeing something inappropriate. We can decide if we will continue to think about it or just move on with our day having better and healthier thoughts.

Tip #2- Double Vow Method

The Talmud (Nedarim 9A) teaches that usually one should not make vows upon himself. However, when it comes to areas of drawing closer to Hashem, such as in striving to become *Shmirat Habrit,* it is highly recommended to make vows that will help him achieve this goal.

Here is a great tip!

First, one makes a vow in front of two witnesses, which makes it binding, that anytime he is about to masturbate, he is required to do something completely irrelevant that will allow him to remove his mind from his inappropriate thoughts.

─THE BATTLE OF OUR GENERATION─

Here are some examples:

a) Go outside for a thirty-minute walk
b) Call someone you look up to & ask for advice on this challenge
c) Leave where you are and sit with your parents for 20 minutes
d) Head to the nearest synagogue and learn for 15 minutes
e) Read a book about the Holocaust for 30 minutes

Then in his vow he mentions that if he does not do one of these and then masturbates, then he should be required to pay a heavy consequence such as $150 to charity or to read the entire book of *Tehilim* (Psalms) in one sitting. However, if he did the irrelevant task first and then masturbated, the consequence will be much milder such as having to only give $10 to charity or having to do 50 push-ups.

The genius of this idea is that when we are in the moment and under the attack of desire, we feel like we need it NOW! However, after the initial peak of intensity, the desire eventually fades. Therefore, if we could distract ourselves with something else and even tell ourselves that we are only taking a break, the desire will eventually fade and we will win that battle.

Additionally, just thinking of the consequences that you will have to face if you give in to your temptations will usually get your mind off the topic and will prevent you from masturbating. Many times people are in doubt if this will work or not but once they actually try it out they realize how amazing it actually is.

----THE BATTLE OF OUR GENERATION----

Tip #3 – Three Second Rule

Another very effective tip is the "Three Second Rule".

Yosef Hatzadik, was placed in an incredibly difficult situation and exercised extreme self-control when the wife of Potiphar in Egypt tried to lure him sexually. We are told that she would change her clothes several times on the daily just to be more alluring to Yosef. On one occasion when nobody was around, Eshet Potifar tried to seduce him. However, Yosef won that battle by quickly running away from the scene.

Why was it so important for Yosef to just **run** away from the scene? Why couldn't he just give it a few moments of thought and discuss the issue with her before fleeing from her presence?

The answer to this question is a crucial and helpful tip when faced with temptation. Yosef understood the power of the *Yetzer Hara*. He knew that if he began to reason with either himself or with her regarding whether or not he should commit the sin, then within mere seconds the *Yetzer Hara* would convince him to act inappropriately with her and justify the action. Therefore, without any time for second thoughts, Yosef quickly ran out of the house and that saved him from doing something that he would truly regret later on.

How do we apply this to our own lives?

The "Three Second Rule" teaches us that we cannot begin to reason with the *Yetzer Hara*. The Yetzer Hara knows us inside and out and it will cause us to sin unless we **quickly and completely** reject it.

For example, if one is on his computer searching for directions to a specific venue and out of nowhere a picture of an immodest woman pops up, he can use the "three second rule" to defeat this temptation. Within the first three seconds, this person can make the

----THE BATTLE OF OUR GENERATION----

most logical decision whether he wants to click on it and continue to see more or instead to close the page and win that battle.

When one sees that first image his emotions don't play such a big roll; however, the *Yetzer Hara* causes him to sin by taking him down gradually, one step at a time. The *Yetzer Hara* will convince the person that by looking at just a couple of more images, it will cause no harm whatsoever. After looking at a few more of those inappropriate images, the *Yetzer Hara* will cause him to look at those images for a few more minutes. After looking at those images for a few more minutes, the *Yetzer Hara* will throw him down yet another step.

Thus, the more this person waits and does not stop looking at these images, the more he will think emotionally as opposed to logically. After a while, his mind will start to make justifications in order to convince him to continue to look at these images. One begins to make justifications like, "I'm sure this sin isn't that bad" or that "The Rabbis probably just made this all up."

The point is that justifications don't come quickly and this person would never have made these justifications during the first three seconds when he saw the first inappropriate clip. Every person has a very small window of time before the Yetzer Hara begins to play tricks on his mind. Once the emotions take over it is significantly more difficult to make an intelligent decision. This is why it is so critical to make a smart decision within the first three seconds just like Yosef Hatzadik did when the wife of Potifar tried seducing him.

Make the right decision in the first three seconds and you will have easily won the battle with the *Yetzer Hara!*

——THE BATTLE OF OUR GENERATION——

Tip #4- Torah, the Greatest Antibiotic!

Hashem implanted the inclination and desire to sin into each and every human being to challenge them. However, Hashem wants us to succeed so much that He even gave us the cure to the problem. The Talmud teaches, "בראתי יצר הרע, בראתיו לו תורה תבלין" (*Kiddushin 30b*). This means that G-d created an infection in our bodies called the *Yetzer Hara* (evil inclination), which constantly pulls us to sin; however, He also gave us the antidote, the perfect antibiotic, to cure ourselves. This antidote is the learning of Torah.

This can be explained through a parable. There was once a man who placed a bandage on the wound of his son saying, "My boy, so long as this bandage is on the wound, eat and drink what you like, hot or cold, and have no fear. But if you take it off, you will get a nasty boil!" This parable compares the evil inclination to a wound on the body. The bandage on the wound signifies the Torah, which protects us and lessens the power of the evil inclination so that we are not deceived by it, causing us to sin. When it goes on to say that you can eat and drink what you like, it means that so long as a man occupies himself with the Torah, even though he surrounds himself with the pleasures of this world, he will not come to transgress, for the Torah will protect him like a bandage on a wound. If, however, he does not occupy himself with the Torah, he is highly prone to "injury".

The Talmud also teaches that, "If the evil inclination confronts you, drag it to the House of Study, for there it is harmless. If it be hard as a rock, it shall smatter; if it be brazen as iron, it shall be broken into pieces." (Kiddushin 30b). There are countless stories about different people who would run to the nearest synagogue or pull out a *Sefer* when they were hit by temptation.

Rav Shlomo Wolbe Zt'l was one of the greatest leading figures of the Jewish world in his generation. Throughout his life, he served as Mashgiach and Rosh HaYeshiva of different institutions in Israel. Many of his tens of thousands of students stand at the

----THE BATTLE OF OUR GENERATION----

forefront of Jewish leadership today. His penetrating words and deep understanding of the human psyche made him a very sought after figure. Students, teachers, Rabbis, and therapist from around the world would travel to him to seek his advice regarding all different types of issues, be it personal, marital, or child related.

In his Sefer, *Alei Shor* (Section 1- Page 40), he points out that we are just one small link connected to a long chain of lineage that dates back over 3,300 years. Thus, it is our responsibility that the links that will follow us in the chain will continue to be strong. We have to strengthen ourselves in every facet of our lives in order to make our link stronger and thereby increase the chances of our descendants staying strong. One important way of achieving this is through putting the appropriate time and effort to work on ourselves and eradicate any problem of lust we might have.

Rav Wolbe also teaches that, "There is no better advice in the world to rule over one's *Yetzer Hara* than learning Gemara (Talmud) with Rashi and Tosafot with an established schedule and persistence." There is something inherently special about Torah which makes it function as the strongest antibiotic possible to battle the evil inclination.

In *Avot D'Rabi Natan* (Chapter 20), Rabbi Chanina Segan-HaKohanim says: "Anyone who puts the words of Torah on his heart will be spared from thoughts (and concerns) of war, thoughts (and concerns) of hunger, thoughts of foolishness, thoughts (and desires) for *Zenut* (lust), thoughts of the *Yetzer Hara*, thoughts (and desires) for married woman, thoughts of nonsense...etc. As it says in the verse in Tehillim (chapter 19 verse 9), 'The laws of Hashem are upright, gladdening the heart; the command of Hashem is clear, enlightening the eyes.'" We see from here that Torah makes the heart happy and frees one's heart from thoughts of negativity that the *Yetzer Hara* occupies it with. The reverse may also, G-d forbid, be true in the sense that if one does not put the words of Torah on his heart, he will be burdened with worrisome thoughts along with an increased temptation.

──THE BATTLE OF OUR GENERATION──

Furthermore, Rav Wolbe adds that, "There's no person who is joyous and fresh as the one who works hard on his Torah study and desires growth. Such a person is aware of his evil inclination but he is better prepared to rule over it and to not allow himself to be ruled by it." He goes on to differentiate between a life void of structure and order (*hefkerut*) and a life of Torah where there is order and meaning. All the physical worldly pleasures, which are temporary, will fail to provide any real satisfaction or meaning for one who does not have Torah in his life. Once those pleasures die out, they tend to leave him feeling even emptier than before.

Therefore, if one sets established times during the day to learn Torah, he will surely see major improvements in his battle with the *Yetzer Hara*. For those who aren't able to learn the Talmud on their own, they should turn to the thousands of lectures available on a vast selection of different topics online. Turn the car rides into something meaningful and productive by playing Jewish lectures. Listen to lectures while you eat or exercise. Here are five of the most popular websites to listen to Torah lectures: www.TheShmuz.com, DivineInformation.com, YUtorah.org, LearnTorah.com, and TorahAnytime.com, which are all available for FREE!

Tip #5 – Prayer

Prayer is a very powerful tool. Chazal teach us that whenever someone needs anything, he should turn to Hashem and speak, in his own words and language, and beg Hashem to grant him that necessity. If this is true of our physical needs it is certainly true of our spiritual needs. Overcoming lust is a critical spiritual need.

Daily prayer to Hashem to help us overcome all of our temptations can be incredibly helpful. It is a great *Nachat* (pleasure) to Hashem when we ask Him for help. He is the one who has given us the challenge and He is the one who can help us win the battle. However, He wants us to beseech Him for it first. Praying an extra thirty seconds for success in this area at the end of the *Shemona*

----THE BATTLE OF OUR GENERATION----

Esreh can be extremely helpful as it shows Hashem that we are desperate to overcome our temptations.

In Alcoholics Anonymous they speak about "Turning to a Higher Power." This is an idea that Judaism has been trumpeting for thousands of years! Hashem is called an Almighty God. He is capable of performing even the greatest miracles and is certainly capable of aiding us in overcoming our lust. Turn this belief into action. Pray to Hashem often and in your own preferred language to help you overcome this battle.

Tip #6 – Internet Filters

Rabbi Yosef Veiner of Agudas Yisrael said, *"I hate to sound pessimistic, but if you have unrestricted internet in the house, internet that is both unfiltered and unmonitored, there's higher than a 90% chance that people have already been Nichshal (stumbled) in that house. And if it hasn't happened yet, there's more than 90% chance it will happen. And if it's not happening at home, it's happening in the office."*

It is extremely important to set up Internet filters on your computers! A computer with Internet is a very powerful tool and it is also a very powerful weapon. Just as a gun has a safety to prevent accidents, so too a computer can be filtered to protect us from making a tragic error.

One can and certainly should also block ads, pop-ups, and flash banners from appearing. One FREE website that is fast and easy to use is https://adblockplus.org

The moment of temptation is very difficult to overcome. In your moments of strength, choose to be strong for the future when you know that strength will be difficult to come by. Fortunately, there are many filters today that are capable of blocking inappropriate websites, without hindering our ability to surf the web in a productive fashion. One such filter is the K-9 web protection. (Here is the link: http://www1.k9webprotection.com)

----THE BATTLE OF OUR GENERATION----

Tip #7 – Seeing Where we Fall

Another successful and helpful tip is to be aware of our vulnerabilities. Once we know our weaknesses, we can set up preventive fences around those weak points to protect ourselves from any future failure. The Pasuk in Mishlei teaches, "*Yodeah Tzadik Nefesh Be'hemato*," which translates to, "A righteous person knows the nature of his animal." We all have an animal inside of us, our challenge is to control it.

To learn what fences we need to make, we have to start asking ourselves how the evil inclination has been so successful until today. How does it get us to fall? How do our minds work in the various situations we find ourselves in? In what habitual ways have we learned to scan our surroundings? Which scenarios trigger our lust the most? What moods are we in when it happens and in what situations do we begin to slip? These are just a few examples of important questions that we need to be asking ourselves in order to conquer our lust.

Take a pen and paper and write down circumstances where you have fallen prey to pornography and masturbation in the past. Try to answer the questions from above in full detail. As you do this, you will notice that there are some common denominators between each time that you stumbled. After seeing all this on paper, you should create a real game plan as to what fences you need to immediately make so you can succeed in the future.

For example, a person may realize that he usually commits this sin between the hours of 4:00pm and 6:00pm, as this is the time that he is always home alone. For this person, the solution would be to find a way to stay occupied during that time by either going out to the park, doing homework in the library, playing ball, or hanging out with friends. What ever this person can do to stay away from being alone during that time is truly worth it.

━━THE BATTLE OF OUR GENERATION━━

Everybody's situation and circumstances are different and that is why everyone needs to do this research on his own and come up with a personalized game plan.

Study your past so you can know how to best strengthen yourself for the future!

Tip #8 – Stay Away From Boredom

Chazal teach us that boredom leads to this sin.

When a person is bored, his mind automatically starts wandering to thoughts of impurity. Until a person purifies his mind and teaches himself to control his thoughts, these thoughts of impurity can become quite commonplace.

It is important to make a schedule and stick to it. Lack of structure creates free time and boredom. Make goals; big or small, spiritual or ordinary. Put energy into reaching those goals in order to be structured and busy. Our Sages teach that a busy schedule with both Torah and work prevents sin. (Pirkei Avot 2:2)

Many young men find themselves with nothing to do. This boredom can often lead to masturbation. The key is to stay active! Fill up your time with productive activities. Take a job, learn Torah, get a hobby, do anything to keep yourself busy! The main thing is to remember that boredom can be dangerous.

Tip #9- Accountability

All too often we keep our sins to ourselves. In general, this may be appropriate. Religion is a private business. However, when it comes to the sin of masturbation it is critical to get help. Keeping this sin in the dark does not fix the problem. We need to be open about our lust and talk to someone about it in an attempt to get help.

----THE BATTLE OF OUR GENERATION----

The Gemara (Kiddushin 81a) recounts a story about Rav Amram *Chasida* (the pious one). Many captive women from war were brought to his house and Rav Amram was fearful of confronting the *Yetzer Hara* while alone. He quickly ran to his roof and began to yell, "Fire at the house of Rav Amram! Fire at the house of Rav Amram!" Moments later, the entire city had gathered at the house of Rav Amram. Now, no longer alone, Rav Amram felt more confident to overcome any possible temptations. It is very clear that Rav Amram was a firm believer that it's better to be embarrassed in this world than in the next world.

Rav Amram was a person with incredible *Yirat Shamaim* (Fear of God) and he still did not feel safe to battle the evil inclination on his own. He knew that unless others would come to his help, he would be no match for the *Yetzer Hara*. Are we really so stubborn and arrogant to think that we are stronger than Rav Amram? In light of the corrupt and immoral nature of our generation, it is foolish to think that we will succeed where men as great as Rav Amram were concerned about failure. If Rav Amram saw fit to create a situation of accountability, then we too need to involve others to aid us in winning these battles.

One suggestion would be to arrange a partnership with someone else who is struggling in the area of *Shmirat Habrit*. Set a goal (such as 20 days, 40 days, 90 days...etc) and work together to achieve that streak. You can motivate each other and pick each other up when you fall. When temptation hits, call your partner and beat the temptation together. Your partner might occasionally fall himself but at that moment where you will need him, he will most likely have a more clear vision of the ultimate goal than you will. He can remind you of your commitment and persuade you not to sin. It is possible that he won't be able to tell you anything new but hearing it from someone else is often a very powerful tool.

----THE BATTLE OF OUR GENERATION----

Inappropriate Dreams

Many people ask what about wet dreams? Am I held accountable for those?

The answer is that it **depends.**

We are only responsible for that which we can control. Did you go to the beach and look at all the women and then consequently, you had a wet dream that week? Did you look at inappropriate things prior to the night of your wet dream? Did you have impure thoughts before your wet dream? If yes, then you are absolutely held responsible for this wet dream and it is as if you purposely wasted seed. The reason is because our dreams are only a result of the thoughts and actions we have while we are awake. In this case, it was surely no accident!

However, if one controls the places he goes to and is careful about the things he chooses to look at, then he is not held responsible for accidental emissions that might occur during his sleep.

The Steipler (Rav Yaakov Yisrael Kanievsky) says that regardless of fault, someone who has a seminal emission should go to the *Mikvah* when possible to be purified.

Additionally, the Halachah is that a person should never sleep on his stomach or back but rather on his side. (Shulchan Aruch, Even Haezer 23:1-3)

One who wakes up and realizes that he had a nocturnal emission should wash his hands and say with a broken heart: "Master of the universe, I did this unintentionally, only from bad feelings and bad thoughts, therefore may it be Your will before you, O Lord my God, and God of my fathers, to erase with Your many mercies this iniquity, and save me from bad feelings and the like forever. Amen! May it be Your will." (Shulchan Aruch 151:5)

----THE BATTLE OF OUR GENERATION----

A True Inspiring Story

Someone that I am close with told me this story about himself:

At the age of 17 he felt that he wanted to better control his lustful temptations and to work on the traits of *Shmirat Habrit* and *Shmirat Einayim* (monitoring what he looks at). He fought this battle and eventually, after many struggles, conquered his temptations. Upon turning twenty-five years old, he found his future wife and was ready to marry her.

He was not a wealthy man and was forced to make a very simple wedding. After the *chuppah,* they danced to the *Yichud* room and when they were finally alone, he looked into his wife's eyes and said, *"Perhaps you are saddened that you didn't get the expensive ring from me as some of your friends received from their husbands. I know that our wedding does not feature the finest catering, the hottest band, or blooming flowers like many others do. However, I do have one very valuable gift that I am prepared to give to you now. In the past eight years, I have been Shomer Habrit and was extremely careful to not look at anything immodest. I am entering this relationship without any addictions or fantasies."*

Upon hearing those words, she broke out in tears of happiness. He explained that at that moment he felt like the richest man in the world. Twenty-Six years later this bride and groom are still happily married and have a very strong and meaningful relationship. A young man's decision to work on his *Shmirat Habrit* and *Shmirat Einayim* made an enormous impact on his future.

Who does not honestly want to give such a precious gift to their wife? What better gift can we give to our wives than to be able to say that we have conquered our lust and are ready to devote our life just to her? A husband who enters a marriage having mastered both *Shmirat Habrit* and *Shmirat Einayim* has in truth supplied his partner with the greatest riches possible and is likely to have a much more meaningful relationship. This is certainly true from a religious perspective and also according to modern day research in psychology.

----THE BATTLE OF OUR GENERATION----

How Pornography Damages Relationships

Psychological issues such as anxiety, low self-esteem, and depression are often the results of keeping our challenges hidden from the light of day.

After years of exhaustive research, top researchers such as Dr. Sennings Bryant and Dr. Dolf Zilman, have concluded that there is no benefit to masturbation. In fact, masturbation has been proven to cause significant physical, social, and mental damages to the person and can negatively affect his family as well.

Research shows that six out of seven women feel that the male's expectations of sex are unreasonable. Women are competing with actresses that have been surgically enhanced, airbrushed, and photo-shopped. Men who expose themselves to pornography and masturbation expect their wives to act exactly as those in the movies. This is obviously an unreasonable expectation and the destructive impact on the marriage is unfortunate.

Additionally, studies indicate that women report feeling betrayed, devastated, and angry when they find out that their husbands watch pornography. They blame themselves for not being "good enough" for their husbands. It often also leads to a lack of trust in the relationship that is very difficult to earn back.

One Cannot Completely Hide From the Yetzer Hara.

Someone once mentioned to me that he is forgoing college, as he knows that he cannot control himself when he gets home after being around so many scantily dressed women. We have to try our best to avoid any tough situations that might put us at risk of sinning. However, not everyone can completely remove himself from the world in such a way.

Thus, the greatest success will come when one works on himself because even if he stops going to school, one can't completely hide from the Yetzer Hara. The *Yetzer Hara* will eventually meet him either at work or on the streets. Living anywhere in the world today, there is a very high chance that you will see something that is inappropriate every single day. However, as one exercises his "self-control muscle" it grows and makes him stronger to ultimately win the battle. One can work on himself to a point where even if he did see something immodest, he still has enough self-control to not look back or reflect on those thoughts.

How Severe is the Sin of Wasting Seed According to the Torah?

Unfortunately, some people assume that wasting seed is not such a significant prohibition according to the Torah. Some people might even consider it just a mere stringency. However, the truth is that anybody who has studied the Torah's perspective on this issue can most definitely attest to the fact that this is a serious matter. The Holy Sages expound on the severity and consequences of this sin in many places. Those who desire to gain a greater perspective on the severity of this sin (from a Torah perspective) should look up the many sources on this topic.

It is important to keep in mind that all of the punishments and consequences for wasting seed and for watching immodest material only apply to one who does not do proper *Teshuva* (repentance). If one does real, sincere *Teshuva*, then he will also merit that all of his previous sins will be taken away.

----THE BATTLE OF OUR GENERATION----

Teshuva- Repentance

Rashi in his commentary on the Torah (Shemot 34:6-7) states that if someone says, "I will not repent because Hashem will not accept my repentance," we tell that person to review the episode of the Golden Calf. *B'nei Yisrael* had just seen the open miracles of the 10 plagues, the splitting of the sea, and Hashem saving them from the Egyptians. Yet, when they were seemingly at the climax of inspiration, they committed perhaps the worst sin in the history of the Jewish people. However, Hashem, who epitomizes mercy, forgave *B'nei Yisrael*. Similarly, if one were to transgress the violation of spilling seed, Hashem will forgive him as long as that person sincerely tries to repent. However, Chazal teach that one who says, "I will sin and then do Teshuva," the Teshuva is no good. (Yoma 85b)

The best way to repent for having committed this sin of wasting seed or having watched pornography is for one to continuously work on himself in order to be victorious in his future personal battles. God is patient; however, one has to be constantly putting in the effort. After each time one loses the battle of *Shmirat Habrit* or *Shmirat Einayim,* he should, for example, add another filter to his computer or take it upon himself to learn about *Shmirat Habrit* for an additional 10 minutes. This shows Hashem that he is doing sincere *Teshuva* and that he really wants to win this battle once and for all.

It is brought down in the *Sefer Menucha v'Kedusha,* written by a student of R' Chaim Volozhiner, that even a person who sins his whole life can still be considered a Tzadik, as long as he never gives up and always continues to fight. We like to think of success in terms of results. But Hashem looks at our efforts in addition to the results.
Over the years many people have attempted to become *Shomer Habrit* and have failed. But, failure is not the end of the story. You can and must pick yourself up and try again. Take an inventory of what went wrong in the past so you can correct those habits for the future. Perseverance and willpower are two very powerful tools.

----THE BATTLE OF OUR GENERATION----

The ultimate goal is to become *Shomer Habrit* forever.

Our Sages taught: *"The Torah cannot be upheld, only through one who has stumbled in it first."* (Gittin 43a) Failure is part of the struggle. When we fall, we learn how to make better fences, create better strategies, and ultimately lead more sanctified lives. Chazal say that Hashem even caused David Hamelech to stumble with Batsheva, only to show us the incredible power of *Teshuvah*.

Hashem, the all-knowing, knows that this is by far the most difficult battle of our generation and that we live in a society that preaches immorality. However, He wants us to fight in order to achieve greatness and earn eternal reward.

Rabbi Nachman of Breslov also revealed a powerful rectification of Shmirat Habrit called Tikkun HaKlali. It is made of 10 Psalms: 16, 32, 41, 42, 59, 77, 90, 105, 137, and 150. Rabbi Nachman promised that these specific 10 Psalms have a special power and should be recited often to rectify this sin that one has committed in the past.

It is also brought down that another way to repent for this sin is through charity. This is true even more so if the charity is given to a relevant cause such as helping others win this battle. (Sefer Hamidos, Niuf 41)

One can repent and accrue great merit if he donates to this organization which uses all the funds solely to help those struggling in these areas.

If you would like to be a partner in this mission please contact:

Phone number: (470) Fight-18 / (470)-344-4818
Email: TheBattleOfOurGeneration@gmail.com
Or Visit us at: TheBattleofOurGeneration.com

——THE BATTLE OF OUR GENERATION——

Depression is Very Dangerous

Almost everyone struggles with lust on some level. Rav Wolbe Zt"l in his famous book "Psychiatry and Religion" (Pg. 82) writes: *"The difficult phase of adolescence is fertile soil for feelings of guilt, especially for religious youth. Masturbation is a serious prohibition. Yet almost all youth stumble with this and are unable to find the strength to overcome this in any way. The result is feelings of guilt."*

When one fails in this area, the *Yetzer Hara* may attack him with a very powerful weapon, guilt. It begins to convince him, "You already broke your streak, just do it again!" Unfortunately, this phenomenon occurs very often. People who have been strong for many months will fail once and then will totally unravel many more times that same week. Why is it that a person can go clean for many months and then once he fails but one time, does he then masturbate numerous times soon after? The answer is that the *Yetzer Hara* convinced him that since he failed once, he is now wicked, and should therefore continue to sin because he will never really win the battle!

Guilt is different than regret. Guilt will paralyze you. Regret will help you think of ways to prevent this from happening again. Guilt leads to depression and once you fall into the trap of depression, the *Yetzer Hara* will convince you to masturbate again and again.

Making it a Top Priority

The importance of *Shmirat Habrit* and *Shmirat Einayim* is universal. Expert psychologists and religious leaders all agree that this is the main challenge of our generation. We need to prioritize this battle if we are to have any real chance of being victorious.

----THE BATTLE OF OUR GENERATION----

One needs to constantly be **proactive** in fighting this battle. Nothing worthwhile comes without hard work. One of the greatest obstacles that prevent a person from changing is that he thinks he can change without putting in the hard work. However, the only way one can change is by actually investing his time to utilize the 9 tips mentioned on pages 18-31 or any other strategies that works for him. One thing is for sure; this problem will not get fixed by itself.

The Vilna Gaon (Sefer Yonah 4:3) explains that every reincarnated soul has one major job to fix upon its return to this world. That trait that he must rectify in his reincarnated state is the trait that he failed at fixing in his previous life. How can we know what our soul's purpose is in this world? The Gaon answers that we can figure it out by observing which sins we stumble upon the most and which sins we have the most intense desire for. For many people in this generation, this is the battle of guarding one's eyes from watching immodest material and abstaining from wasting seed.

Human nature is to seek what is easy and comfortable and avoid inconveniences. In that way we are no different than animals. Animals don't understand that a painful experience can be beneficial – try to explain surgery to a cow! Pleasure and suffering are both a part of life but we get to choose which pleasures and sufferings we want. The choice is either the very short and temporary physical pleasure that lust offers us, which comes with huge side effects, or the pleasures that Hashem wants us to have, which are infinitely greater. It is difficult at first, but when one can overcome this battle, it becomes his most valuable asset.

There are some things that we truly need such as food, water, and sleep. Our *Yetzer Hara* tries to convince us that other things such as wasting seed is also a necessity. As one works on himself, he realizes that not only is masturbation not a necessity but that he could survive and actually live a much more meaningful and productive life without it.

----THE BATTLE OF OUR GENERATION----

There is a famous Pasuk that says, *"Seven times does the righteous one fall and get up" (Mishlei, 24:16).* Rav Hutner expounds this verse to mean that it does not mean "even after falling seven times, the righteous one manages to gets up again." Rather, it means that it is only and precisely *through* repeated falls that a person truly achieves righteousness. The struggles – even the failures – are inherent elements of what can, with determination and perseverance, become an ultimate victory.

Hashem wants to reward us with infinite Divine pleasure and He gave us a beast inside of us to slay. Hashem could have made us as mighty as the angels who are without temptation. However, it is through human beings who desperately fight the battle in the darkness of this world that allows them to grow spiritually and achieve greatness.

How Do These Behaviors Lead to Addiction?

It's simple neuroscience! Just like with any pleasure, the pleasure sensory pathway is stimulated in the brain. Whether it's marijuana, cocaine, alcohol, or the pleasure one might get from inappropriate scenes viewed during a movie, the serotonin levels spike and the pleasure pathways are activated in the standard "addiction" pattern.

As a matter of fact, masturbation behaviors have been shown to be more powerful and addictive than most drugs. Masturbation's intense pleasure stimulation is even more direct than hard drugs and upon repeated exposure to certain types of stimulation, one tends to seek out even more perverse and intense stimulation. This ends up leading to that vicious self-destructive cycle that is typical of addictions.

----THE BATTLE OF OUR GENERATION----

How it Alters the Brain

It wasn't long ago that doctors and researchers believed that in order for something to become addictive and detrimental to somebody, it had to be an outside substance that you physically put into your body like cigarettes, alcohol, or other drugs. However, modern day research shows that this statement is false and internal struggles can become addictive as well.

Cocaine and pornography don't seem to have much in common. One is purchased on the black market and can become very expensive over time; the other, pornography, is both free and can be accessed so easily with just one click. However, leading experts in the field have proven that mentally, the harm of drugs and pornography are very similar. (Doidge, N. (2007). New York: Penguin Books, 106)

A few years ago a famous scientist, Jim Faust, performed an experiment with rats. Rats are appalled by the smell of dead carcasses. Faust gathered virgin male rats and put them in the same cage as the female rats. He then sprayed the female rats with the horrible dead carcass scent that they are highly disgusted by. The experiment showed that the sexual drive of the rat was so high that it overpowered its instinct to avoid the dead rat smell and the rats ultimately mated.

Later, Faust placed toys that were sprayed with this exact dead rat smell and since the rats had associated that horrible smell with sexual pleasure they engaged with the toys.

What caused these rats to go against their natural instinct of being disgusted with the dead carcass smell? The answer is dopamine. The dopamine that was released when these rats were involved in sexual activity was so high that the rat's brain associated the pleasure of dopamine's release with the dead rat smell. Thus, the dead rat smell became something that was associated with pleasure.

----THE BATTLE OF OUR GENERATION----

Both rats and humans have the same reward pathways in the brain. The rat's preferences were rewired in their brain in the same way that **pornography rewires the human brain**.

Dr. Jeffrey Satinover of Princeton University said regarding pornography, *"It is as though we have devised a form of heroin 100 times more powerful than before, usable in the privacy of one's own home, and injected directly to the brain through the eyes."*

The good news is that neuroplasticity works both ways. This means that the damage to the brain can be undone when someone abstains from pornography and masturbation for a period of time.

Additionally, we all have something in our brain called the "reward pathway." Its function is to reward us with a chemical called dopamine when we do certain things that give us pleasure. When one watches pornography his brain gets flooded with a really high level of dopamine. A healthy brain isn't used to all that dopamine, so the brain responds by getting rid of some of its dopamine receptors. However, when the body reacts with fewer receptors, the person can no longer feel the same excitement or arousal from that type of pornography. As a result, they have to watch more porn, watch it more often, and move to more intense material to feel that same original feeling. What happened? The answer is that the brains pleasure response has gotten numb.

Additionally, since the dopamine receptors were reduced, this person can no longer feel the same normal pleasures anymore. Little things that once made him happy like seeing a friend or playing a good sport, might not be able to make him happy anymore because now he has less dopamine receptors, which results in less pleasure. Pornography can easily give one the illusion that it increases pleasure, however, it comes at the great expense of a reduction in our long-term pleasure. (Angres, D. H 2008 and Journal of Adolescent Health 27, 2: 41–44.)

----THE BATTLE OF OUR GENERATION----

Erectile Dysfunction

Thirty years ago, when a man developed ED (Erectile Dysfunction), it was almost always because he was getting older (usually over 40 years old). It was unheard of anyone under 35 years old getting diagnosed with Erectile Dysfunction. However, that was before pornography met the Internet. Today, Erectile Dysfunction is eight times more prevalent than thirty years ago, and it has nothing to do with age.

Let's give an example to explain the reason for this. Imagine going to the most extreme theme park in America and riding a very intense roller coaster numerous times. By the 10th time, no matter how scary and crazy of a thrill it was, the roller coaster loses its excitement. It becomes boring and you need a more intense roller coaster to give you a thrill.

The same is true with pornography. At first when a person watches something inappropriate the feeling of arousal is sudden and intense. As time goes by those "basic clips" no longer give him that same feeling of pleasure. More intense material is necessary for arousal. With time he keeps moving on to more and more intense material until he reaches a point where almost nothing can get him aroused anymore. When this man gets married, his wife will be nothing to him compared to those fake models he flooded his brain with. Reaching this point of not being able to be aroused by most things causes Erectile Dysfunction, which so many men are affected by today.

What most people don't understand is that a short pornography scene can take longer than several days or weeks of filming. However, it leaves the viewer with the impression that everything just happened without break and that it will be very similar to his sexual experience. Additionally, when watching pornography if something doesn't immediately satisfy somebody, he can quickly switch it to the next image or video within a second. However, in a real marriage we cannot do that.

----THE BATTLE OF OUR GENERATION----

Important to Keep in Mind

1) With each ejaculation a man loses 300-400 million spermatozoa. Each sperm has the potential of creating a child, a new human in this world. Kabbalisitically, each one of the 300-400 million spermatozoa are holy and can cause spiritual damage when wasted.

2) People who masturbate often have a much higher chance of becoming sexually impotent by the age of 40. (Harvard Medical School, Men's Health)

3) Another terrible result of wasting seed is that it desensitizes us to a spiritual connection. The more we sin in this area, the more desensitized we become. This is a commonly experienced phenomenon, where people slowly lose their yearning for spirituality and they start to feel ever more disconnected from Torah, Shabbat, and Mitzvot.

4) Hashem created a world that functions with a system of free will. If there were no free will, then there would be no significance to any good deed one performed. For instance, if Hashem would strike someone with an illness every time he violated Shabbat, people would become so afraid of the punishment that they would memorize every rule of Shabbat. However, Hashem does not want us to be like a robot and just serve him out of fear of being punished or in order to just receive reward. He wants it to be out of love and connection! What is more meaningful: A gift you receive from someone who was forced to give it to you, or a gift from someone who gives it to you because he or she deeply wants to?

Similarly, when it comes to the area of *Shmirat Habrit*, Hashem does not want to remove our free will. Therefore, He hides the immediate punishments of wasting seed. However, this does not mean that Hashem does not take note of this matter or that the punishments do not exist.

The rewards are also not immediate. If we were able to clearly see the rewards that we receive every time we pass the test and hold ourselves back from looking at something inappropriate or from wasting seed we would be in shock and truly amazed.

Japan-Herbivores

Studies have shown that those who have an addiction to masturbation tend to feel less of a desire to get married. Additionally, those who are already married but have a masturbation problem tend to not be as interested in sexual intimacy with their wives because they feel that they can just pleasure themselves. There is a very interesting, yet, sad example of this in Japan.

When the population rate in Japan started rapidly decreasing, researchers became curious to investigate the matter. After much research, the link became very obvious. Japan has the highest rate of pornography watched per capita out of all the countries in the world. The researchers found that the people in Japan have gotten so addicted to pornography that they feel no need to get married. A new trend has developed in Japan where the men have been remaining single and childless because they seem to find no purpose in getting a wife when they can just pleasure themselves. As a result, Japan has had a major decline in their population rate. (Breitbart: "Japanese Population Decline Due to Porn.")

One of the consequences of pornography and masturbation is that it decreases the desire of single men to get married and it reduces already married men's desire for intimacy with their wife. This has become such a popular topic in Japan that those who are victims of this epidemic are now called the "Japan Herbivores".

——THE BATTLE OF OUR GENERATION——

Marriage is Not a Hospital!

Many people believe that they will be able to masturbate until they get married and then it will be easy to stop. But that's not the case; the more one masturbates, the more difficult it becomes to stop. Masturbation does not have a switch that can just be easily turned off the night before one's wedding.

Rabbi Twerski says, "It's important to know that the addiction should be put under control before considering marriage. Marriage is not a hospital and does not cure the addiction and continuation of the addiction is likely to ruin the marriage."

Unfortunately, there are many men who continue to watch pornography and even masturbate when they are married. As mentioned earlier, it is very common that a wife will catch her husband. All the marriage counselors can attest to the fact that from then on, after being caught, there is a cheapening of the marriage coupled with a lack of trust that can even lead to divorce.

Unless one actually puts in the effort to stop, this can turn into a continuous problem existent throughout ones life. It can severely hurt him, his wife, and even his children.

No Excuses

The Talmud teaches that when one leaves this world not having conquered his temptations for lust, he will not be able to give any excuses. He will be asked, "Why didn't you spend more time and effort in order to conquer your temptations and stop this sin once and for all?" The Gemara proceeds to say that one will not be able to answer, "My *Yetzer Hara* was too strong and I was not able to, no matter how much I tried." If he does attempt to answer in such a way, he will be asked, "Was your *Yetzer Hara* stronger than Yosef Hatzadik's *Yetzer Hara*, who had the strongest *Yetzer Hara* possible pushing him to sin all those times?"

If Yosef conquered his *Yetzer Hara*, then our *Yetzer Hara*, which is less powerful, definitely can be conquered with determination and perseverance. Although it might be difficult, it is definitely not impossible. Therefore, we will not be able to use any excuses when we leave this world and stand before judgment.

Some Extra Bonuses

We are told that when someone has the opportunity to look at something that is inappropriate but he refrains from doing so, Hashem announces in Olam Haba "So and so is a *Tzadik*" and Avraham, Yitzchak, Yaakov, and Moshe all ask, "who is this person?" Suddenly, all the righteous people in the next world become very curious and want to know more about him. It is brought down that for a minute, he is like Yosef Hatzadik and the great merit gained through his self-control gives him a very strong power of *Tefillah* (prayer).

The Steipler Rav promised three things if one is *Shomer Habrit:*

1) For every pleasure that a person denies himself solely because the Torah forbids it, he will ultimately receive that pleasure in a permissible way.

2) He draws an unfathomably large and awesome holy light and at that moment he is on the level of Yosef Hatzadik.

3) He merits Divine assistance in all endeavors, success in Torah study, and character improvement.

––––THE BATTLE OF OUR GENERATION––––

Power of 90

Often people worry about how they will be able to erase all those dirty images their brains got flooded with from when they had not yet overcome this challenge. However, there is much hope! A recent scientific study found that it takes 90 days to change the neuron pathway in the brain. It was shown that if a person refrains from their addictive behavior for 90 days then they would find it much easier to stop the addictive thought patterns.

It is interesting, but like usual, *Chazal* knew this way before scientists. There is a *Halacha* (rule) that after Ashkenazim change in *Shemona Esreh* from "Vaten Tal Umatar Livrahca" that if someone is in doubt whether or not he remembered to make the switch, then he only repeats the entire prayer if it has been less than 30 days since the change took place. However, if it has been over 30 days then he does not need to repeat it.

Why is 30 days so significant? The answer is that when a person prays 3 *Tefilot* a day for 30 days that equals 90. *Chazal* knew this special power of 90 when it comes to memory even way before the scientist did. So if one wants to know how to eliminate all those dirty images he put into his mind, the answer is that after he stops they will slowly fade and by the 90th day, the person will have much cleaner thoughts.

Additionally, it's interesting that the *Gematriah* (numerical value) for the letter "Tzadik (צ)" which represents a Tzadik (righteous person) is also 90.

––––THE BATTLE OF OUR GENERATION––––

It's Worth so Much!

Within the Torah, there are 613 commandments. Of those 613 commandments, 365 of them are negative commandments for which the punishments are clearly delineated. The other 248 are positive commandments for which we are NOT told of the rewards associated with them (besides the two exceptions).

Why does the Torah tell us the punishments for breaking any one of the 365 commandments but yet it does not tell us the reward for the performance of the positive commandments?

The answer to this question is that the reward for a mitzvah is dependent on more than the mere performance of the mitzvah. The circumstances, difficulty, effort, etc… are all taken into account. For instance, a businessman who is required to be at the office by 7:30am with an hour commute will have to be finished with *Minyan* by 6:30am. This may mean waking up as early as 4:30am in order to make a 5:15am *Minyan*. Another person may find himself in a situation where he does not need to arrive at work until 10am. His neighborhood might even have a plethora of *Minaynim* allowing him to pray at the *Minyan* of his choice. Can we say that the man who had to put true *Mesirat Nefesh* (sacrifice) in order to pray with a Minyan and the person who had it easy will have the same reward after 120 years? Obviously Not!

The same principle can be applied to *Shmirat Habrit*. Some people have an easy time conquering their temptations while many others find it extremely challenging to. Those who find it difficult to control their lust and yet still desperately try to win, will be rewarded in much greater proportion. Additionally, compared to other *Mitzvot*, the pain and effort required is much greater, and the reward is therefore proportionally much greater as well. This concept is also mentioned in Pirkei Avot as the Mishna teaches, "Lefoom Tzarah Agrah"- "According to the pain is the reward."

----THE BATTLE OF OUR GENERATION----

Additionally, Chazal teach that, "A *Mitzvah* done one time with suffering is more valuable than one done a hundred times without suffering."

Think About it – is it Worth it?

The pleasure experienced when one masturbates is temporary. Yet, the consequences are life lasting and effect one physically, mentally, and spiritually. The question everyone must ask themselves is: "am I willing to sacrifice so much for just mere seconds of temporary pleasure?" There is no better feeling than knowing that you are no longer a slave to your desires.

It is important to keep in mind that while the beginning of the battle with *Yetzer Hara* may be difficult it eventually becomes tremendously easier. The difficulty involved in this incredible battle will eventually fade away and just become a natural part of life. A lot of times people are afraid that there will always be the same level of difficulty in fighting masturbation. However, this is a totally false belief. The greatest difficulty in this area is definitely in the beginning but after that its gets much easier. Many Tzadikim say that the first 40 days are the most difficult and then the battle becomes significantly easier.

Knowing that the difficulty will only be for a short period of time and then you'll have a much easier time, should be strong motivation for anyone to commit himself to become *Shomer Habrit*.

The Talmud (Sukkah 52b) teaches us a very important fact: **"There is an organ in man, if one feeds it, it will remain hungry, but if one starves it, it will be satisfied."** This means that the more one commits this sin, the more difficult it will become to stop. However, if one holds back from committing the act, it becomes tremendously easier to overcome the temptation in the future.

----THE BATTLE OF OUR GENERATION----

As a Jew, knowing the Torah's view on this sin ought to be enough to get us to stop sinning. But if it is not, there is also the additional motivating factor to stop spilling seed for your own well-being and for the well-being of your future wife and children.

Why do you think the Torah restricted such behavior in the first place? Does Hashem gain anything by making our lives less enjoyable or more burdensome? Obviously Not!

Hashem created us and He knows all about our bodies pleasure system. Hashem wants us to have the most pleasure in the best way possible. Sometimes that means sacrificing the here-and-now temporary pleasure in order to enjoy the long lasting and more meaningful pleasures. We know the word Torah comes from the word *Hora'ah*, which in Hebrew means 'instruction'. Hashem has given us the instructions on how to live the most meaningful and productive life. Thirty-three hundred years after the Torah was given, we see that the secular world is catching up to the Torah and are making claims that agree and support what Hashem instructed us to do!

―――THE BATTLE OF OUR GENERATION―――

Conclusion

If you just finished reading this book and all you can say is, "That was interesting" and just move on with your life without internalizing the messages conveyed here, then to some degree I have failed and perhaps the several thousands of hours I spent on this book was wasted.

Inspiration is temporary! Please do not expect that because you read this book one time that you will still be inspired in two weeks from now. Read this book again and again!! Life cannot be lived passively. If you truly want a better life you have to be proactive and constantly commit to change.

In 5 minutes it may already be too late as your inspiration may have already dwindled. So for your own sake: take something upon yourself **NOW!!** Perhaps implement one of the many tips recommended in this book. Install a filter block on all your electronics.

You have seen the facts and learned the tips – the decision is now yours! I really hope that you will make the right choice so that you and your family will live a life filled with the greatest blessings, *Shalom Bayit*, self-confidence, happiness, and closeness with Hashem for eternity.

----THE BATTLE OF OUR GENERATION----

Extra Information

The following is all brought down in the *Sefer Taharat Hakodesh* in the name of the *Zohar Hakodesh*:

- The entire world was created and exists because of those who are Shomer Habrit. *(Bereishit 56a, Tikkunim 64b)*
- When *B'nei Yisrael* is Shomer Habrit, no other nation can rule over them. (Bereishit 66b)
- It is as if you kept the entire Torah if you are Shomer Habrit. (Bereishit 193a; Vayikra 13b)
- Someone who is Shomer Habrit has the *Shechinah* constantly in his presence both in this world and the next. (Lech Lecha 94b)
- If a person is Shomer Habrit properly, he is called a "MIGHTY" warrior. (Beshalach 61b)
- If a person is Shomer Habrit, Hashem himself heals that person both physically and spiritually. (ibid)
- Hashem rejoices every day over the people that are Shomer Habrit. (Shelach 165b)
- A person who is Shomer Habrit is called a Tzadik just like Yosef, who was Shomer Habrit. (Bereishit 59b; Vayera 53a)
- When Hashem sends energy down to the world it first passes through the people that are Shomer Habrit. (Bereishit 162a)
- One that is Shomer Habrit merits that to have holy children that will guard themselves. (Lech Lecha 93b)
- The Angel Duma stands at the entrance of *Gehinom* (hell) along with thousands of afflicting angels. They are not allowed to harm those that were Shomer Habrit in this world. It also says in Gemara Eruvin that Avraham saves those who are Shomer Habrit from Gehinom. (Eruvin 19a)
- When Mashiach is revealed, there will be much destruction in the world; however, those that are Shomer Habrit will be saved. (Tikkuney Zohar 54b)

----THE BATTLE OF OUR GENERATION----

- *Ayin Hara* (evil eye) has no control over a person who guards his eyes. (Tikkunim 28a)
- It is only possible to attain the attribute of humbleness if one is Shomer Habrit.
- Someone who is Shomer Habrit merits that he is given the opportunity to do many uncommon Mitzvot and Tikkunim. These mitzvoth are normally hard to come across.
- Someone who is Shomer Habrit will attain a level where he is constantly in a state of happiness.

----THE BATTLE OF OUR GENERATION----

Bibliography

In addition to reading and mastering this book, I highly recommend reviewing some other very relevant and practical material. These following five sources were so powerful and helpful that I often referred to them and quoted them within this book.

1)Keeping Holy: A compilation of letters gathered from the Steipler (Rav Yaakov Yisrael Kanievsky) which discuss the importance of *Shmirat Habrit* (protecting oneself from wasting seed).

2)GYE- There is an amazing organization called 'Guard Your Eyes'. They are always available to help anyone with their hotline, daily *Chizuk* emails, Internet filters, and their wide variety of other resources. They also have a very well known eBook available for free. Visit them at GuardYourEyes.com or call them at (646)-600-8100.

3)Fightthenewdrug.org – This is a completely non-Jewish organization that has been established to combat pornography. Even many of the secular non-Jews have come to the clear conclusion that pornography is severely detrimental in many different ways. I advise everyone to learn more about the topic by visiting their website and reading their many books on this topic.

4) Holy Nation by Lehavas Hatorah

5) You Shall Be Holy by Breslov

----THE BATTLE OF OUR GENERATION----

Inspiration is Contagious!

Unfortunately, everybody knows at least one person who is truly struggling in this battle. It is now your responsibility to spread the light and help them become victorious. Please get a copy of this book into their hands and motivate them to read it cover to cover. (If you need more copies please contact us).

We would also like to hear your comments and opinions on this book. Please email us your feedback so we can make improvements for later editions.

Our organization is completely non-profit and our objective is to inspire Jews across the world to fight this battle against pornography and masturbation.

Please donate, as it would be a great merit for you and a big help for us to continue our many programs.

Call: (470) Fight-18 / (470)-344-4818

Email: TheBattleOfOurGeneration@gmail.com

Or Visit us at: TheBattleofOurGeneration.com

www.ingramcontent.com/pod-product-compliance
Lightning Source LLC
Chambersburg PA
CBHW071800040426
42446CB00012B/2647